UNSHAKEN

Finding God's Strength When Life Trembles

EMANUEL WALKER

Copyright © 2025 The Walker Effect

All rights reserved. No part of this book may be reproduced or transmitted in any form or by any means, electronic or mechanical, including photocopying, recording, or by any information storage and retrieval system, without the author's written permission, except for the inclusion of brief quotations in a review.

Scriptures taken from the New International Version (NIV). PPNIV®. Copyright © 1973, 1978, 1984, 2011 by Biblica, Inc.™ Used by permission of Zondervan. All rights reserved worldwide. www.zondervan.com The "NIV" and "New International Version" are trademarks registered in the United States Patent and Trademark Office by Biblica, Inc.™

Scripture quotations marked (NLT) are taken from the Holy Bible, New Living Translation, copyright ©1996, 2004, 2015 by Tyndale House Foundation. Used by permission of Tyndale House Publishers, Carol Stream, Illinois 60188. All rights reserved.

Scripture quotations are from the ESV® Bible (The Holy Bible, English Standard Version®), © 2001 by Crossway, a publishing ministry of Good News Publishers. Used by permission. All rights reserved. The ESV text may not be quoted in any publication made available to the public by a Creative Commons license. The ESV may not be translated in whole or in part into any other language.

Scripture taken from the New King James Version®. Copyright © 1982 by Thomas Nelson. Used by permission. All rights reserved.

For permission requests, please get in touch with the author at www.emanuelwalker.com

ISBN: 979-8-9986641-2-0

*To my mother, **Oretha Zaybay**—who sacrificed everything to bring us to America in hopes of a better life. Your courage is the foundation of every opportunity I've had.*

*To my grandparents, **the Scotts**—who mentored me and nurtured my relationship with God when I needed it most.*

*To my brothers in arms—**Augustine, Rick, Brandon, Sed, Lavar, Montay, and Mason**—thank you for keeping me grounded, humble, accountable, and hungry for more.*

*To my God-given mentors—**Angie, Jermaine, the Coburns, Gerald, Otis, and Medo**—each of you taught me something essential, right when I needed it. You didn't just show up—you spoke life.*

*And above all, to the **God who never let go**—even when I was ready to give up. May this book reflect Your faithfulness more than my own.*

"The LORD himself goes before you and will be with you; he will never leave you nor forsake you."
— (Deuteronomy 31:8, NIV)

Foreword

In a world that trembles with uncertainty, many search for something firm to stand on—something that won't shift beneath the weight of pain, loss, or disappointment.

I know that search well.

I've stood at the edge of failure—with a 1.6 GPA and no hope of college. I've packed bags for a dream school, only to be sent home, defeated. I've served in conflict zones, faced frozen marches, and carried burdens far heavier than my rucksack.

Through every storm—from refugee camps to boardrooms, pulpits, and battlefield briefings—I've discovered one enduring truth: **God is faithful when everything else fails.**

Unshaken is not a collection of abstract thoughts. It's a book forged in the fire of adversity, anchored in Scripture, and wrapped in the rawness of real life. Each devotional was born from a moment when I had to choose between fear and faith, discouragement and resilience, despair and hope.

This is for the one who's still fighting, still questioning, still standing—barely. Whether you're walking through broken relationships, shattered dreams, vocational uncertainty, or spiritual silence, my prayer is that these pages remind you: there's a Kingdom that cannot be shaken and a God who never lets go.

Let these stories be your companion.

Let these Scriptures become your song.

And may this devotional not just inspire you—but help you rebuild your foundation, one day, one promise, one prayer at a time.

With faith that still stands,

Emanuel Walker

Contents

Foreword v

SECTION I - Finding Strength In Struggle

From Rock Bottom to Redemption 3
The Frozen March 5
The Valley of Shadow 7
When Plans Crumble 9
Strength in Weakness 11
Invisible Growth 13
Learning to Fail Forward 15

SECTION II - Anchored In Faith

Anchored in the Storm 19
When God Seems Silent 21
Beauty from Ashes 23
Anchored in Chaos 25
The Loving Push 27
Beauty in Broken Places 29
The Sacred Silence 31

SECTION III - Walking In Community

Finding God in the Wilderness...33
The Mirage of Solo Faith..37
Resilience Through Relationships..39
First Steps Without Footprints...41
Legacy of Horizons...43
From Fury to Peace..45

SECTION IV - Embracing Divine Purpose

Bigger Than Your Circumstance...49
The Invisible Guide...51
Second Chances..53
Unusual Callings...55
Unlikely Open Doors...57
Misplaced Faith..59
Courage for One More Step...63

SECTION V - Cultivating Daily Faithfulness

Small Steps, Big Journey...67
The Rhythm of Rest..69
The Unseen Workout..71
The Gift of Disruption..73
Horizons Beyond Home..75

About the Author..77

SECTION I
Finding Strength in Struggle
Theme: Overcoming Hardships, Discovering God's Power in Weakness

From Rock Bottom to Redemption

But he said to me, 'My grace is sufficient for you, for my power is made perfect in weakness.

2 CORINTHIANS 12:9 (NIV)

I still remember staring at my 1.6 GPA on that wrinkled report card, my stomach sinking with the realization of how far I had fallen. As a refugee who came to this country with dreams of success, I found myself failing—not because I couldn't succeed, but because I had lost my way.

That moment became my turning point. Sometimes, God allows us to hit rock bottom so we have nowhere to look but up. My academic failure wasn't just about grades—it reflected a life without direction or purpose.

The journey from that 1.6 GPA to eventually becoming valedictorian wasn't immediate or easy. It required daily choices, consistent discipline, and most importantly, surrendering my future to God. He didn't just want to fix my grades—He wanted to transform my character.

Paul's words in 2 Corinthians remind us that God's power shines most visibly through our weaknesses. When we come to the end of our resources, we create space for His unlimited provision. When we admit our inadequacy, we position ourselves to experience His sufficiency.

What area of your life feels like rock bottom today?

God doesn't waste our struggles. Your current weakness might be the very place where His strength will be displayed most magnificently.

Prayer:

Lord, transform the areas in my life where I feel like a failure into testimonies of Your grace. Help me remember that my lowest points can become the foundation for Your greatest work in my life. In Jesus' name, Amen.

The Frozen March

I can do all things through Christ who strengthens me.

PHILIPPIANS 4:13 (NKJV)

U.S. Army Air Assault School—also known as "the 10 hardest days in the Army."

Air Assault School pushed me to my physical limits, but nothing compared to the 12-mile ruck march on that bitter winter morning. As I stood at the starting line in the pre-dawn darkness, my breath formed clouds in the freezing air. I surveyed what lay ahead—twelve miles of snow-covered terrain, a 40-pound rucksack on my shoulders, and an M4 rifle growing heavier by the minute.

Two miles in, I discovered that all my water had frozen solid. By mile four, icicles had formed on my rifle. My muscles screamed for hydration, for rest, for warmth. Each step became a decision to continue—despite every physical indication that I should stop.

In those moments of extreme physical challenge, I experienced what Paul meant when he wrote, *"I can do all things through Christ who strengthens me."* This verse isn't a spiritual magic wand that makes difficulties disappear. It's the profound truth that when our strength ends—when water freezes, when muscles fail, when the mind wants to surrender—Christ's strength becomes accessible in ways we can't explain.

I completed that march in under two hours—not because I was the strongest soldier, but because I tapped into a strength beyond my own. The frozen march taught me that our perceived limitations are often just that—perceptions. With Christ's strength, we can push beyond what we thought possible.

What challenge are you facing that seems beyond your strength?

Remember that Philippians 4:13 isn't about what you can do, but about what Christ can do through you when you surrender it all to Him.

Prayer:

Lord, when my strength fails and I want to quit, remind me that Your power works beyond my human limitations. Help me draw on Your strength rather than depending solely on my own resources. In Jesus' name, Amen.

The Valley of Shadow

Even though I walk through the darkest valley, I will fear no evil, for you are with me; your rod and your staff, they comfort me.

PSALM 23:4 (NIV)

Psalm 23 is one of the world's most beloved scriptures, yet its profound comfort never diminishes with repetition. David's imagery of *"the darkest valley"* (or *"the valley of the shadow of death"* in some translations) acknowledges a universal human experience—seasons of deep darkness, danger, and dread.

What makes this verse so powerful is not that it promises exemption from dark valleys. David acknowledges the reality of walking *"through the darkest valley."* But he emphasizes two truths that transform how we experience these inevitable passages.

First, valleys are places we move through—not places where we permanently reside. The darkest valley has both an entrance and an exit. Your current suffering, no matter how overwhelming, is not your final destination.

Second, we never walk these valleys alone. *"You are with me"* may be the most important phrase in the entire psalm. God's presence doesn't remove the valley, but it fundamentally changes our experience within it. We are accompanied by the Shepherd whose rod defends and whose staff guides.

Notice that at this point in the psalm, David shifts from talking about God (*"He leads me"*) to talking **to** God (*"You are with me"*). Our darkest valleys often become the places where God's presence becomes most personal.

If you're in a dark valley today, hold tightly to these twin truths: this valley is temporary, and you are not alone in it. Keep walking, one faithful step after another, knowing the Shepherd walks beside you.

Prayer:

Lord, in the valleys I go through, help me sense Your presence beside me. Remind me that those dark places are not destinations, but merely a path to deeper relationship with You. In Jesus' name, Amen.

When Plans Crumble

Many are the plans in a person's heart, but it is the LORD's purpose that prevails.

PROVERBS 19:21 (NIV)

I still remember the day I packed my bags for Oklahoma, my heart full of dreams.

College represented everything I had been working toward—my ticket to a better future. A local church had promised to fund my scholarship, and I felt God's hand guiding my path forward.

Then came the phone call that changed everything.

The church refused to sign off on the scholarship they had promised. Just weeks into my new beginning, I was forced to drop out and return to Colorado—defeated, lost, and completely hopeless.

I found myself working in a nursing home kitchen, scraping food off plates, wondering if this was what God had planned for me all along. The future I had so carefully mapped out had crumbled before my eyes.

Perhaps you know this feeling.

The job offer falls through.

The relationship ends.

The medical diagnosis arrives.

The financial support disappears.

And suddenly, the path you were certain God wanted you to walk vanishes beneath your feet.

Proverbs 19:21 offers profound wisdom for these moments:

"Many are the plans in a person's heart, but it is the Lord's purpose that prevails."

It acknowledges our natural tendency to make plans—a reflection of being made in the image of a Creator God. Yet it gently reminds us that our plans are always subordinate to God's greater purpose.

What I couldn't see in that nursing home kitchen was that God was preparing me for something better.

That disappointment led me to the Community College of Denver. During my first week, I wore a suit—something small, but it caught the attention of the Vice President, who would later become my mentor. Through that *divine appointment*, God set me on a path that eventually led to graduating at the top of my class and receiving high-level job offers—opportunities that never would have come if my original plans had worked out.

When plans fail, we face a critical spiritual decision:

Will we respond with resentment, questioning God's goodness?

Or will we meet the disruption with faith, trusting that His purposes remain intact—even when ours fall apart?

Prayer:

Lord, I surrender my plans to You. Give me eyes to see Your goodness in the midst of my disappointments. Help me remember and trust that Your divine purpose will prevail, even when my life takes unexpected turns. In Jesus' name, Amen.

Strength in Weakness

That is why, for Christ's sake, I delight in weaknesses, in insults, in hardships, in persecutions, in difficulties. For when I am weak, then I am strong.

2 CORINTHIANS 12:10 (NIV)

Paul's declaration in 2 Corinthians 12:10 presents one of the most counterintuitive principles in Scripture. **Delighting in weakness** runs contrary to everything our achievement-oriented culture celebrates. We're taught to hide our weaknesses, overcome them, or at least compensate for them—certainly not to **delight** in them.

Yet Paul goes beyond mere acceptance of weakness to actual **delight**. This isn't masochism or false humility—it's a profound recognition that his weaknesses created space for Christ's power to be displayed. The areas where Paul couldn't rely on his own strength became the very places where divine strength was most visibly manifested.

This paradox echoes throughout Scripture:

- **Moses**, who struggled with speech, became God's spokesperson.
- **Gideon**, the least in his family, led Israel to victory with a drastically reduced army.

- **David**, the overlooked shepherd boy, defeated Goliath.

In each case, human weakness became the canvas for divine strength to shine through.

Our weaknesses—whether physical limitations, personality quirks, traumatic histories, or lack of natural talent—are not obstacles to God's work but **opportunities** for it. They keep us dependent on Him, humble instead of proud, and grateful rather than entitled.

What weakness are you trying desperately to hide or overcome? Consider how it might actually be creating space for God's power to move in your life in ways that strength never could.

Prayer:

Lord, I bring my weaknesses before You. Rather than hiding my limitations, help me see them as channels for Your power. Transform the areas where I feel inadequate into showcases for Your perfect strength. In Jesus' name, Amen.

Invisible Growth

Do not despise these small beginnings, for the LORD rejoices to see the work begin.

ZECHARIAH 4:10 (NLT)

My academic turnaround didn't happen overnight. For months, I studied diligently without seeing significant improvement in my grades. Late nights, early mornings, weekends sacrificed—yet the results seemed disproportionately small compared to my efforts.

Growth is often invisible before it becomes undeniable. Like a seed pushing beneath the soil, the most important development happens where no one sees.

In those discouraging moments, I learned to trust the process God had me in. Every vocabulary word memorized, every math problem solved, every paragraph written—none of it was wasted, even when immediate results weren't visible.

Zechariah 4:10 offers a profound reminder not to "despise small beginnings." This verse was originally spoken to the Jews rebuilding the temple after exile. The foundation they laid seemed pitiful compared to Solomon's magnificent temple. But God delighted in their faithfulness with what they could do—not in their ability to produce immediate, impressive results.

Transformation happens in the hidden moments of faithfulness.

The daily disciplines that no one applauds often produce the fruit everyone eventually celebrates. The prayers prayed in private eventually manifest in public blessing.

Where in your life are you working without seeing results?

Don't underestimate what God is doing beneath the surface. Those small beginnings—consistent prayer, Scripture reading, fasting, and showing up when it's hard—are laying the foundation for significant growth.

Prayer:

Lord, when I'm tempted to grow discouraged by slow progress, remind me that You delight in faithful beginnings. Help me build patience and trust in Your plan for my life. In Jesus' name, Amen.

Learning to Fail Forward

Though the righteous fall seven times, they rise again.

PROVERBS 24:16 (NIV)

My first speaking engagement was a disaster. I froze halfway through, forgot my carefully prepared words, and stumbled off stage feeling humiliated. The easy choice would have been to never speak again.

But God doesn't call us to avoid failure—He invites us to **fail forward**. That painful experience taught me more about public speaking than any success ever could. It exposed weaknesses I needed to address and ignited a determination to grow.

Resilience isn't about avoiding falls—it's about how quickly you get back up. The righteous person in Proverbs doesn't fall just once, but seven times. The distinguishing factor isn't the falling—it's the rising.

This proverb reveals a profound spiritual truth about the nature of righteousness. A righteous person isn't someone who never fails—they're someone who refuses to stay down. Their righteousness isn't displayed in perfection, but in persistent faith that leads to repeated rising.

Throughout Scripture, we see this pattern:
- **Abraham** failed in faith, yet rose to become the father

of nations.
- **David** fell morally, yet rose to be called a man after God's heart.
- **Peter** denied Christ, yet rose to lead the early church.

Their legacies weren't defined by their falls, but by their **faith-filled determination to rise again**.

What failure has left you hesitant to try again?

Remember—your worth isn't determined by your performance. Some of God's greatest work happens in the space between our failures and our courage to begin again.

Prayer:

Lord, help me see my failures as opportunities for growth rather than reasons to quit. Give me the courage to rise again when I fall. In Jesus' name, Amen.

SECTION II
Anchored in Faith
Theme: Finding Stability Amid Life's Storms

Anchored in the Storm

We have this hope as an anchor for the soul, firm and secure. It enters the inner sanctuary behind the curtain, where our forerunner, Jesus, has entered on our behalf.

HEBREWS 6:19–20 (NIV)

The ancient world understood the critical importance of anchors. Without modern navigation systems or engines, ships at sea were entirely vulnerable to winds and currents that could drive them onto rocks or sweep them into the open ocean. A reliable anchor wasn't a luxury—it was a necessity for survival.

The writer of Hebrews uses this powerful metaphor to describe Christian hope. This isn't wishful thinking or optimistic sentiment. Biblical hope is a confident expectation based on God's character and promises—an anchor that holds firm regardless of the storms surrounding us.

What makes this anchor uniquely reliable? It doesn't merely grip the seabed of human circumstances or philosophical ideas. It extends into the very presence of God—"the inner sanctuary behind the curtain." Our hope is anchored in heaven itself, where Christ has already gone before us.

When storms of doubt, grief, confusion, or fear threaten to overwhelm your faith, remember that your soul is anchored not to shifting sand but to the immovable reality of God's throne room. The line connecting you to that anchor might feel stretched and strained, but it cannot break—because Christ Himself secures it.

Hope anchored in anything less than God will ultimately disappoint. Careers end. Relationships change. Health declines. Economies fluctuate. But hope anchored in Christ's finished work and God's faithful character provides stability that transcends circumstances.

Prayer:

Lord, when storms threaten to overwhelm my faith, anchor my soul firmly in Your unchanging presence. Help me remember that while the waves may rise and fall, my hope is secured to Your eternal throne—not to shifting circumstances.

In Jesus' name, Amen.

When God Seems Silent

The LORD is close to the brokenhearted and saves those who are crushed in spirit.

PSALM 34:18 (NIV)

There were nights throughout my journey when my prayers seemed to hit the ceiling and bounce back. Studying for hours yet failing tests. Non-stop training, missions, and periods of isolation. Giving my best, yet seeing little improvement. In those moments, God felt distant and silent.

Perhaps you're in a season where heaven seems quiet. Your prayers feel unheard. Your circumstances remain unchanged despite your faithful petitions.

But the silence of God doesn't equal the absence of God. Sometimes His most important work happens in the quiet—like a farmer who plants seeds and must wait patiently through silent seasons of growth beneath the soil.

It reminds me of the book of *Esther*, which remarkably never mentions God's name even once—yet His fingerprints are visible on every page through the "coincidences" and perfect timing that save His people. In the apparent silence, God was orchestrating redemption behind the scenes. Our lives often follow this pattern—what appears to be divine silence is actually sacred orchestration.

Psalm 34:18 offers profound comfort during these silent seasons.

It doesn't promise instant deliverance from brokenheartedness or crushed spirits. Instead, it promises God's closeness in the midst of those painful experiences. His presence may not always be felt, but it is guaranteed—especially to those experiencing deep pain.

The incarnation itself testifies to this truth. In Jesus, God entered human suffering rather than removing it from a distance. His closeness to the brokenhearted became literal as He experienced betrayal, rejection, physical pain, and even spiritual abandonment on the cross. He knows what it means to cry out, *"My God, why have You forsaken me?"*

If God seems silent in your life right now, remember—His closeness is promised, especially to the brokenhearted. Keep praying, keep seeking, keep trusting—even when the answers aren't immediately visible.

Prayer:

Lord, when things seem silent, help me trust in You. Like in the story of Esther, even if I don't see it, You're written all over my circumstances. Give me faith to trust in Your works, even when I can't see or feel them. In Jesus' name, Amen.

Beauty from Ashes

To all who mourn in Israel, he will give a crown of beauty for ashes, a joyous blessing instead of mourning, festive praise instead of despair.

ISAIAH 61:3 (NLT)

Have you ever watched something precious to you turn to ashes?

Perhaps it was a relationship you invested years in building. Maybe it was a career that once defined your identity. Or possibly a ministry you poured your heart into—only to see it suddenly collapse.

Isaiah's prophetic promise speaks directly to those mourning such losses. The imagery is powerful: *ashes* represent complete destruction—the final state of something burned beyond recovery. Yet, God specializes in taking what appears completely destroyed and creating something beautiful from it.

This isn't merely about positive thinking or making the best of a bad situation. It's about recognizing that God's redemptive power can transform our greatest losses into platforms for His glory. The cross itself—an instrument of torture and shame—became the ultimate symbol of salvation and hope.

Transformation rarely happens overnight. The journey from ashes to beauty often includes seasons of deep, genuine mourning. God doesn't rush us through grief or minimize our pain. But neither does

He leave us in that place permanently.

Where do you see only ashes in your life today?

A dream that died?

A mistake that seems irredeemable?

A loss that feels permanent?

Bring those ashes to God—with honesty about your pain and openness to His redemptive work. The beauty He creates may look different from what was lost, but it will carry a glory the original never could have contained.

Prayer:

Lord, I bring You the ashes in my life, trusting Your promise to create beauty from them. Help me remain patient in the transformation process—neither denying my grief nor losing hope in Your redemptive power. In Jesus' name, Amen.

Anchored in Chaos

Jesus Christ is the same yesterday and today and forever.

HEBREWS 13:8 (NIV)

The news flashed another crisis.

Natural disasters, political upheaval, economic uncertainty, global conflicts—each headline seemed designed to provoke anxiety. I found myself being pulled into a vortex of worry, constantly checking updates, allowing each new development to disturb my peace.

Then one morning during prayer, a gentle question formed in my spirit:

"Has any of this changed who I am?"

The question wasn't mine—it felt like God's voice cutting through the noise.

Has any headline changed God's power?

Has any crisis altered His promises?

Has any global event diminished His love?

Hebrews 13:8 reminds us that *"Jesus Christ is the same yesterday, today, and forever."*

This isn't just theological doctrine—it's practical comfort in unstable times. While circumstances, cultures, and conditions constantly change, **our God remains consistent.**

The unchanging nature of God gives us a fixed point in a spinning world. When everything around us seems to be shifting, His character provides solid ground beneath our feet. His promises don't fluctuate with stock markets or election results. His purposes aren't derailed by pandemics or natural disasters.

This doesn't mean we should ignore current events or pretend that suffering doesn't matter. Jesus Himself wept over Jerusalem and felt compassion for the crowds. But He never lost sight of the Father's larger purposes or allowed the troubles of His day to define His reality.

Fixing our eyes on the unchanging nature of God amid chaos isn't denial—it's **spiritual wisdom.** It's choosing to interpret current events through the lens of eternal truth, rather than interpreting eternal truth through the lens of current events.

What narratives are shaping your perception of reality today?

Are you allowing temporary headlines to override timeless promises?

Remember, the God who parted seas, raised the dead, and transformed your heart is **undiminished by today's challenges.** His promise to care for you—in this life and the next—remains as certain as ever.

Prayer:

Lord, as the chaos of current events creates anxiety in my heart, anchor me in Your unchanging character. Help me filter today's headlines through the lens of Your eternal promises rather than interpreting Your truth through temporary circumstances. In Jesus' name, Amen.

The Loving Push

For the Lord disciplines the one he loves, and chastises every son whom he receives.

HEBREWS 12:6 (ESV)

When my mother brought us to the United States as refugees, we arrived with nothing but the clothes on our backs. As a child, I often didn't understand her strictness. While other parents seemed more lenient, my mother pushed me relentlessly toward excellence. Her expectations felt impossible at times, and I questioned why she couldn't just let me be "normal" like other kids.

Years later, additional mentors entered my life—coaches, teachers, pastors—who shared that same tendency to push me harder than others. One coach would make me run extra laps. A teacher would mark my papers more critically. A pastor would question my spiritual commitments more deeply.

"Why are they so hard on me?" I would wonder.

It wasn't until I had achieved things I never thought possible that I finally understood: they pushed because they saw potential in me that I couldn't yet see in myself. Their strictness wasn't cruelty—it was belief. A belief that I was capable of more than mediocrity.

This human dynamic reflects a profound spiritual truth. Scripture tells us that God disciplines those He loves. His correction isn't punishment—it's preparation. His high standards aren't meant to discourage us, but to develop us into who He knows we can become.

Like a skilled sculptor who chips away more aggressively at the marble that will become the focal point of the masterpiece, God often works most intensely on those He's preparing for significant purpose. The areas where you feel His correction most strongly may, in fact, be the areas of your greatest future strength.

Are you feeling the pressure of high expectations? Do you sometimes wonder why God doesn't make your path easier? Perhaps it's because He sees in you what you cannot yet see in yourself—potential worth developing, gifts worth refining, and a future worth preparing for.

Prayer:

Lord, when I face expectations that stretch me, help me recognize them as expressions of belief in what You can do through me. Give me the strength to embrace challenges that develop my character and prepare me for the purposes You've designed for my life. In Jesus' name, Amen.

Beauty in Broken Places

The LORD is close to the brokenhearted and saves those who are crushed in spirit.

PSALM 34:18 (NIV)

The Beauty in Brokenness

The ancient Japanese art of *Kintsugi* fascinates me. When pottery breaks, artisans repair it using gold-infused lacquer, creating something even more beautiful than the original. Rather than hiding the fractures, they highlight them—transforming brokenness into art.

One winter evening, sitting alone, surrounded by broken pieces of what were once certain dreams and expectations, this practice seemed to whisper a spiritual truth to me. My journey hadn't followed the expected path. Relationships had fractured. Plans had collapsed. The neat, unblemished life I had imagined gave way to something more complicated, marked by visible breaks and careful repairs.

Yet in those broken spaces, I began to see God's presence most clearly. The moments that shattered my self-sufficiency became the very places where divine grace poured in—not to conceal my brokenness, but to highlight it with something precious.

Scripture repeatedly affirms that God does His most profound work in broken places. He draws near to the brokenhearted. He gives beauty for ashes. He uses cracked vessels to carry His light. The narrative of redemption itself centers on how the broken body of Christ becomes our healing.

Our culture often treats brokenness as something to conceal. We present curated versions of our lives, filtering out imperfections and struggles. Yet genuine spiritual formation happens not in hiding our fractures, but in surrendering them to the Master Craftsman—who specializes in beautiful repairs.

Your broken places—the disappointments, failures, and wounds you've experienced—aren't disqualifications from God's purposes. They are, in fact, the very spaces where His redemptive work becomes most visible. When we allow God to restore our brokenness, He doesn't simply return us to our original state. He creates something more beautiful, more authentic, and more reflective of His grace than if we had never been broken at all.

What broken pieces are you trying to hide today?

What if those very fractures could become the places where God's light shines most brilliantly through your life?

Prayer:

Lord, I surrender my broken pieces to Your healing hands. Transform my shattered places with Your redemptive touch, making them beautiful displays of Your restoration power. Help me find the courage to be honest about my brokenness rather than hiding behind a façade of perfection. In Jesus' name, Amen.

The Sacred Silence

Guard what has been entrusted to your care. Turn away from godless chatter and the opposing ideas of what is falsely called knowledge.

1 TIMOTHY 6:20 (NIV)

My excitement bubbled over as I shared the news—a promising opportunity, a potential open door, a possible breakthrough.

"God's going to do something amazing," I announced to friends, family, and on social media.

Weeks later, when the opportunity evaporated, I was left not only with disappointment but also with the awkwardness of explaining why my premature announcement had come to nothing.

This pattern repeated itself in my life more times than I care to admit—a job prospect, a ministry initiative, a relationship. I would speak about these possibilities as certainties, only to watch them dissolve. Each time, I sensed God gently teaching me a lesson about the power and purpose of silence.

Scripture repeatedly commends discretion and warns against hasty speech. Jesus often told those He healed not to broadcast their miracles. Joseph didn't announce his divine dreams to the prison guards. Ruth quietly worked in the fields before her redemption story unfolded. There's a sacred wisdom in moving quietly until God indicates it's time to speak.

Why is silence so valuable in our spiritual journey?

First, it protects developing works from premature exposure. Just as a photographer doesn't pull film out in daylight, some divine workings need darkness to develop properly.

Second, it guards our hearts from the distraction of others' opinions. When we announce every divine whisper, we invite a chorus of voices that can drown out God's further instructions.

Third, it keeps our motives pure. Quiet faithfulness is rarely rewarded with applause, helping us serve for God's approval alone.

Finally, it preserves us from the embarrassment of proclaimed victories that never materialize—disappointments that can damage our witness and discourage others.

I've learned to embrace what some spiritual writers call *holy hiddenness*—seasons where God's work in and through us remains largely invisible to others. These times aren't punishment but preparation—not divine withholding, but divine protection.

What is God developing in your life right now that might need the protection of silence?

What passion, project, or possibility might benefit from being held close until the proper time?

Prayer:

Lord, give me discernment to know when to speak and when to remain silent. Help me resist the urge to announce prematurely what You've only whispered in private. Teach me to value the sacred work You do in secret, trusting Your perfect timing for revelation. In Jesus' name, Amen.

Finding God in the Wilderness

I remember you—the kindness of your youth, the love of your betrothal, when you went after me in the wilderness, in a land not sown.

JEREMIAH 2:2 (NKJV)

The wilderness has always been where God does His deepest work.

Moses encountered the burning bush in Midian's desert. Elijah heard God's still, small voice in the cave at Horeb. John the Baptist prepared for ministry in Judea's wilderness. Even Jesus Himself was led by the Spirit into the desert before beginning His public work.

I discovered this truth during a season of profound isolation, after a job transfer took me far from family and community. Weekends would pass without meaningful human interaction. At first, I interpreted this as abandonment—why would a God who created us for community allow such isolation?

Yet gradually, I began to recognize it as an invitation rather than an exile. In the absence of other voices, God's voice became clearer. In the spaces once crowded by activity, prayer expanded. In the silence that initially terrified me, divine whispers became audible.

Jeremiah 2:2 reveals how God views our wilderness seasons—

with tenderness and remembrance: *"I remember the devotion of your youth, how as a bride you loved me and followed me through the wilderness."* The barren landscape stripped away distractions, clarified dependency, and created sacred space for devotion.

Your wilderness may look like emotional desolation, vocational uncertainty, or spiritual dryness. Whatever form it takes, the invitation remains: seek God precisely in the place that seems God-forsaken.

The wilderness is never the destination but always the pathway— to deeper intimacy, clearer calling, and stronger character. Your current desolation may be preparation for your greatest fruitfulness.

Prayer:

Lord, in my wilderness season, help me recognize Your presence rather than just feel abandoned. Open my heart to hear Your voice. Transform what feels like exile into a sacred encounter that deepens my devotion to You. In Jesus' name, Amen.

SECTION III
Walking in Community
Theme: The Importance of Relationship and Mutual Support

The Mirage of Solo Faith

And let us consider how we may spur one another on toward love and good deeds, not giving up meeting together, as some are in the habit of doing, but encouraging one another—and all the more as you see the Day approaching.

HEBREWS 10:24–25 (NIV)

When I first gave my life to Christ, I attempted to walk the journey alone. I read my Bible in private, prayed in isolation, and kept my struggles to myself. I believed that true spirituality was a solitary pursuit—just God and me against the world.

How wrong I was.

After months of struggling alone, I became spiritually exhausted and began to doubt my faith. It wasn't until a persistent church member invited me to a small group that I discovered what I had been missing: **community**.

The author of Hebrews understood something vital about faith: it was never meant to be a solo journey. The early Christians met in homes, shared meals, pooled resources, and carried each other's burdens. They knew that **faith flourishes in community**.

While there are certainly seasons of isolation in the spiritual journey (Jesus Himself withdrew to pray alone), these are meant to be temporary. We need others to:

- Hold us accountable when we're drifting
- Encourage us when we're discouraged

The phrase *"spur one another on"* in Hebrews 10:24 is particularly striking. The Greek word used here, *paroxysmos*, suggests a sharp—even irritating—prodding. True spiritual community isn't always comfortable; it involves **loving confrontation and gentle correction**.

When I finally embraced church community, I found not only accountability but also unexpected blessings. I met mentors who guided me, friends who supported me, and eventually, my spouse. What I initially viewed as an optional add-on to my faith turned out to be **essential to my spiritual growth**.

Are you trying to navigate your faith journey alone? What barriers are keeping you from authentic spiritual community? Remember—even Jesus didn't do ministry solo. He gathered disciples around Him.

Prayer:

Lord, forgive my self-sufficiency that masquerades as spiritual maturity. Help me engage authentically in community—being honest about my struggles and receptive to wisdom from others. Break down the walls I've built that keep people at a distance. In Jesus' name, Amen.

Resilience Through Relationships

Two are better than one, because they have a good return for their labor: If either of them falls down, one can help the other up.

ECCLESIASTES 4:9-10 (NIV)

My journey through military service taught me an essential truth about resilience: it's rarely developed in isolation. During particularly grueling training exercises, it wasn't personal determination alone that kept me going—it was the bonds formed with fellow service members who wouldn't let me quit when every muscle screamed for relief.

Ecclesiastes 4:9–10 highlights this principle of mutual support with pragmatic wisdom. The text doesn't romanticize independence but emphasizes the practical advantage of partnership: "a good return for their labor." When one person falls—physically, emotionally, or spiritually—the other provides essential support.

Scripture consistently emphasizes this communal aspect of perseverance.

- Moses needed Aaron and Hur to hold up his arms during battle (Exodus 17:12).
- Paul relied on Timothy's encouragement during imprisonment (2 Timothy 1:16–18).
- Even Jesus sought the support of Peter, James, and John in Gethsemane (Matthew 26:37–38).

The journey of faith and perseverance was never meant to be traveled alone. God deliberately designed spiritual growth to happen in community, knowing we need others who will speak truth when we're deceiving ourselves, provide perspective when our vision narrows, and offer encouragement when our strength falters.

Who makes up your community of support?

If that circle feels empty right now, what step could you take toward authentic connection? Sometimes, the humility to admit our need for others is the first step toward the resilience God wants to develop in us.

Prayer:

Lord, thank You for the gift of community. Help me be vulnerable enough to receive support and generous enough to offer it to others on their journeys. In Jesus' name, Amen.

First Steps Without Footprints

The LORD himself goes before you and will be with you; he will never leave you nor forsake you. Do not be afraid; do not be discouraged.

DEUTERONOMY 31:8 (NIV)

Being the first in my family to do many things meant there was no well-worn path to follow—no experienced guide to tell me what to expect. Each step—from scholarship applications to internship interviews—was uncharted territory. There were no footprints to place mine within, only fresh snow awaiting first impressions.

The weight of being a trailblazer extended beyond academia. As the first to navigate professional networks, corporate culture, and leadership roles, I often found myself in situations where I had no family blueprint to reference. The question, *"What would Dad do in this situation?"* rarely yielded applicable answers—because my father never faced these challenges.

Perhaps you're in a similar position—the first in your family to pursue higher education, start a business, lead a ministry, or walk with Christ. You've discovered both the exhilaration and the loneliness of forging new paths.

Moses understood this tension. As he prepared to transfer leadership to Joshua, he acknowledged the anxiety of pioneering but also offered a powerful promise:

"The LORD Himself goes before you and will be with you."

This verse contains a fascinating paradox—God goes before us, yet remains with us simultaneously.

For the trailblazer, this is profound comfort. Though we may be the first in our families to walk certain paths, we are never the first in absolute terms. God has already gone before us. He has mapped the territory. He knows every obstacle and opportunity ahead.

At the same time, we're not alone in the present moment. The God who goes before us also stays with us—guiding, strengthening, and encouraging. We may lack human footprints to follow, but we have divine presence to sustain us.

Being a trailblazer isn't about having all the answers or never feeling afraid. It's about moving forward with the confidence that comes from knowing you're never truly forging the path alone. When there's no blueprint except *you and God,* that's actually the most reliable blueprint of all.

Prayer:

Lord, as I walk paths no one in my family has traveled before, remind me that while I may be the first in human terms, You've already gone ahead of me. Give me courage to move forward, trusting that Your guidance surpasses any human blueprint I could follow. In Jesus' name, Amen.

Legacy of Horizons

One generation commends your works to another; they tell of your mighty acts.

PSALM 145:4 (NIV)

The steering wheel felt heavy with responsibility as I drove my younger siblings across the country from Colorado to Florida. Years earlier, I had been the wide-eyed teenager on this same route with my church "grandparents." Now, I was the guide—determined to give my siblings, who had never left Colorado, the same gift of expanded horizons.

We stood at the edge of the Grand Canyon, wandered through Nashville, and dipped our toes in the Gulf of Mexico. At each stop, I shared not just the sights but the stories—how God had been faithful to our family, how He had taken a child from poverty and broadened his world, how the same God who created these wonders was intimately involved in our lives.

Throughout the entire journey—thousands of miles there and back—we experienced remarkable protection. No accidents, no car trouble, not even a speeding ticket. Beyond safety, God seemed to sprinkle little gifts along our path: an unexpected hotel upgrade, a free meal from a kind stranger, perfect weather at key tourist stops.

Psalm 145:4 speaks of how one generation tells another about God's works. This is more than an information transfer—it's a testimony. When we share what God has done, we're not just recounting history; we're inviting others into a living relationship with the One who still acts in history.

I realized on that trip that faith isn't just something we experience individually—it's meant to be transmitted. The blessing I received years earlier wasn't meant to end with me but to flow through me to the next generation. My siblings weren't just seeing America—they were witnessing the goodness of God through the lens of our family's story.

Who is watching your journey?

What younger generation is learning about God through your testimonies? The faith you've received isn't meant to stop with you—it's meant to be passed on, enriched by your own experiences of God's faithfulness.

Prayer:

Lord, help me be intentional about sharing Your faithfulness with others, especially those younger than me. Let my life be a channel of blessing, not a reservoir. Use my stories to draw others closer to You. In Jesus' name, Amen.

From Fury to Peace

My dear brothers and sisters, take note of this: Everyone should be quick to listen, slow to speak and slow to become angry, because human anger does not produce the righteousness that God desires.

JAMES 1:19–20 (NIV)

The basketball slammed against the gym wall as I stormed off the court, fuming after a disagreement with a teammate. As a teenager, anger was my calling card—quick to ignite and destructive in its path. Whether it was a perceived slight, a lost game, or family tension, my response was predictable: explosion.

But my anger wasn't just a personality quirk—it was a wall between me and others, between me and peace, between me and God. I knew it, and in my quieter moments, I prayed desperately for change. "God, take this from me. I don't want to be known for my anger anymore."

The transformation didn't happen overnight. There was no dramatic deliverance moment, no instant personality transplant. Instead, God worked gradually—teaching me through Scripture, through mentors, and through the painful consequences of my outbursts.

James 1:19–20 became my meditation. I wrote it on index cards, taped it to my mirror, and repeated it when I felt the familiar heat rising: "Quick to listen, slow to speak, slow to become angry." These weren't just nice suggestions—they were divine wisdom about how human hearts operate.

Today, people often describe me as "chill" or "level-headed"—descriptions that would've seemed laughable to those who knew me in my youth. The transformation is so complete that new friends sometimes don't believe the stories of my former temper.

This change doesn't mean I've reached perfection. I still have moments when anger rises, when old patterns threaten to reemerge. But God's work in me has created new pathways, new responses, new possibilities.

This is the miracle of sanctification—not that we instantly become perfect, but that God patiently reshapes us to more closely resemble Christ. His perfection works on our imperfection, bringing us ever closer to the people He designed us to be.

What rough edges is God smoothing in your life? What patterns seem so entrenched that you doubt they could ever change?

Remember: the God who formed the universe from nothing can certainly reform your character—one day at a time.

Prayer:

Lord, thank You for Your patient work in my life. Continue transforming the areas that don't reflect Your character. Help me lean on Your Spirit to make me more like You. In Jesus' name, Amen.

SECTION IV
Embracing Divine Purpose
Theme: Discovering and Following God's Unique Calling

Bigger Than Your Circumstance

> *Now to him who is able to do immeasurably more than all we ask or imagine, according to his power that is at work within us.*
>
> EPHESIANS 3:20 (NIV)

When I sat in my high school counselor's office with a 1.6 GPA, college seemed impossible. Graduate school? Unimaginable. Becoming valedictorian or a student leader representing over 137,000 students? Beyond my wildest dreams.

Yet God specializes in writing stories that far exceed what our circumstances suggest is possible. He takes five loaves and feeds thousands. He takes a shepherd boy and raises up a king. He takes a cross—a symbol of shame—and transforms it into the means of our salvation.

Paul's declaration in *Ephesians 3:20* stretches our spiritual imagination: God is able to do not just what we ask, not just what we imagine, but "immeasurably more" than both combined. The Greek word Paul uses here implies something that cannot be measured or calculated—it exceeds our mental arithmetic.

Notice where this immeasurable power operates: *within us.* God's power isn't only displayed through dramatic external events, but also through internal transformation—changed character, renewed minds, healed emotions, restored relationships. Often, the most spectacular miracles are the ones that happen inside us.

Your current limitation is not your final destination. God's vision for your life has never been constrained by your past failures, present struggles, or personal inadequacies. Where you see obstacles, He sees opportunities to display "His power that is at work within us."

Prayer:

Lord, expand my vision beyond my current limitations. Where I see obstacles, help me trust that You see opportunities. Increase my faith to believe that You can accomplish immeasurably more than I could ever ask or imagine. In Jesus' name, Amen.

The Invisible Guide

Trust in the LORD with all your heart and lean not on your own understanding; in all your ways submit to him, and he will make your paths straight.

PROVERBS 3:5-6 (NIV)

The most pivotal decision of my military career came from the most unexpected source.

As a young recruit trying to determine my Military Occupational Specialty, I felt overwhelmed by options. Each path offered different advantages and drawbacks, with lifelong implications I couldn't fully grasp.

After weeks of indecision, I posted my dilemma on an online military forum. A response came from someone I didn't know—detailed guidance about considering not just immediate benefits but also the long-term career trajectory. Something about their wisdom resonated deeply, and I followed their advice to select Military Intelligence.

That decision eventually positioned me for the Green to Gold program, leading to my commission as a Cyber Warfare Officer—an opportunity I never would have accessed through other pathways. When I returned to the forum months later to thank this stranger, their profile had mysteriously disappeared. No trace remained of the account that had so dramatically altered the direction of my life.

I've often wondered if God sometimes works through "angels unaware," sending guidance through unexpected channels when we're humble enough to receive it. Throughout Scripture, God rarely reveals the full roadmap—He illuminates just the next step and asks us to trust Him for the rest.

Proverbs 3:5–6 doesn't promise we'll understand God's guidance in the moment. In fact, it explicitly tells us **not** to lean on our own understanding. The invitation is to trust when the path ahead isn't clear—and to submit, even when the direction doesn't make immediate sense.

Where are you seeking clarity today?

What decision has you paralyzed with uncertainty? Remember that God's guidance often comes in unexpected ways to those willing to listen and obey—even when the full picture isn't visible.

Prayer:

Lord, help me recognize Your guidance even when it comes through unexpected channels. Give me courage to take the next step in faith when I cannot see the entire path. In Jesus' name, Amen.

.

Second Chances

Being confident of this, that he who began a good work in you will carry it on to completion until the day of Christ Jesus.

PHILIPPIANS 1:6 (NIV)

Dropping out of Southern Nazarene University in Oklahoma felt like final proof that I wasn't cut out for higher education. After struggling academically in high school and now failing in college, the pattern seemed clear: I simply wasn't college material.

I carried that identity—*academic failure*—like a heavy weight. Each time I considered trying again, memories of past setbacks flooded my mind. *What made me think this time would be different? How many chances could one person waste?*

But God specializes in second chances. And third chances. And hundredth chances. His grace isn't limited by our track record of failure. When I finally gathered the courage to try again, I approached education with a new perspective—not as something to conquer by my own strength, but as a journey to walk with God's help.

The transformation wasn't immediate or easy. But step by step, class by class—guided by mentors and sustained by prayer—something shifted. The student who once dropped out eventually stood as valedictorian. Not because I suddenly became brilliant, but because God's work in me continued despite the detours.

Paul's words in *Philippians 1:6* offer profound encouragement to anyone tempted to believe their failures disqualify them from God's purposes:

"He who began a good work in you will carry it on to completion until the day of Christ Jesus."

The good work God begins, He commits to completing. Your false starts, setbacks, and stumbles haven't derailed His intentions for your life—they've simply become part of the story of His faithfulness.

Reflection:

What dream have you abandoned because past failures convinced you it was impossible? Consider that God's timeline for your growth may be longer and more gracious than the one you've imposed on yourself.

Prayer:

Lord, thank You for being the God of multiple chances. Help me trust that You're still working in my life despite my failures and detours. In Jesus' name, Amen.

Unusual Callings

For we are God's handiwork, created in Christ Jesus to do good works, which God prepared in advance for us to do.

EPHESIANS 2:10 (NIV)

"Why are you wasting your time with that?"

The question came from a well-meaning friend as I invested hours into a creative project that seemed disconnected from my main responsibilities. It wasn't the first time my pursuits had been questioned.

Throughout my life, I've felt drawn to activities and interests that others found puzzling. From obscure sports to unconventional hobbies, my passions often lay outside the mainstream. For years, I second-guessed these inclinations, wondering if they were distractions rather than callings.

What I've discovered, however, is that God places these desires in our hearts for purposes beyond what we can initially see. That unusual sport? It led to relationships with people I would never have met otherwise—people who needed to hear about God's love. That quirky creative project? It opened doors to share my faith in environments where traditional ministry would never have gained entry.

Ephesians 2:10 tells us we are God's handiwork—His poem, His masterpiece (the Greek word is *poiēma*)—created for specific good works He planned long ago. This means our unique interests, talents, and even our peculiarities are not accidents, but divine design elements.

The Bible is filled with people whose unusual skills became platforms for God's work: Bezalel's craftsmanship, David's musicianship, Lydia's business acumen, Paul's tent-making. None of these were traditionally "spiritual" skills, yet God used each one powerfully.

What passion has God placed in your heart that might seem odd to others? Instead of suppressing it or dismissing it as impractical, could you ask God to show you how it might serve His purposes? The very thing others question might be the unique tool God wants to use in your life.

Don't let conventional expectations limit how you serve God. The kingdom advances not just through traditional ministry roles, but through the infinite variety of giftings God has distributed among His people.

Prayer:

Lord, thank You for the unique passions You've placed within me. Help me see how these can be used for Your glory, rather than dismissing them as unimportant. Show me the unexpected ways You want to work through my distinct design. In Jesus' name, Amen.

Unlikely Open Doors

See, I have placed before you an open door that no one can shut.

REVELATION 3:8 (NIV)

I still remember staring at that job posting for a Business Analyst internship at a major software startup.

The requirements seemed to mock my qualifications: advanced Excel skills, project management familiarity.

With only my associate's degree from a community college in hand, I hesitated to even apply. Everyone else would surely have bachelor's degrees from prestigious universities—or even be graduate students. *Who was I to think I belonged in that room?*

But something inside urged me forward.

During the interview, when asked about specific technical skills, I could have pretended or exaggerated. Instead, I simply told the truth:

"I don't have many of these skills yet, but I'm willing to learn anything you need me to."

To my astonishment, I received the offer for this highly paid internship. Walking into orientation confirmed my fears—I was indeed the only one with just an associate's degree. Everyone else came from prestigious universities or graduate programs with impressive pedigrees.

What happened next can only be explained as *God's hand at work*. Not only did I quickly learn the necessary skills, but I inadvertently became the intern team lead. My unique background and perspective allowed me to approach problems differently. By the end of the internship, I had made a remarkable impact on both the company and my peers—me, someone who was totally unqualified. **Because of God.**

God's open doors rarely look like what we expect. Throughout Scripture, we see this divine pattern:
- Joseph's imprisonment became his path to leadership.
- David's shepherd background prepared him for kingship.
- Paul's status as a former persecutor gave him unique credibility in preaching grace.

What I perceived as disadvantages, God used as qualifications for the very door He was opening. His criteria for opportunity differ dramatically from the world's. Where humans see disqualification, God often sees distinctive preparation.

Are you standing before a door that seems impossibly closed based on your qualifications?

Remember Revelation 3:8—when God opens a door, no human standard, academic requirement, or past failure can shut it. The very experiences you consider disadvantages might be precisely what God will use.

What opportunity seems beyond your reach today because you feel unqualified?

Take one small step toward it this week, trusting not in your abilities but in God's power to work through your willingness.

Prayer:

Lord, help me recognize the doors You're opening, especially when they don't match my expectations. Thank You that my limitations never limit You. Give me courage to walk through open doors even when I feel unqualified, knowing that Your strength is made perfect in my weakness. In Jesus' name, Amen.

Misplaced Faith

When Jesus saw him lying there and learned that he had been in this condition for a long time, he asked him, 'Do you want to get well?' 'Sir,' the invalid replied, 'I have no one to help me into the pool when the water is stirred. While I am trying to get in, someone else goes down ahead of me.' Then Jesus said to him, 'Get up! Pick up your mat and walk.' At once the man was cured; he picked up his mat and walked.

JOHN 5:6-9 (NIV)

The Pool of Bethesda: When the Healer Stands Before You

The scene at the Pool of Bethesda reveals one of the most profound interactions in Jesus' ministry. Here was a man who When Jesus, the Creator of the universe and source of all healing, stood directly before him and asked, *"Do you want to get well?"* the man couldn't see beyond his fixation on the pool.

Notice his response. He doesn't say, *"Yes, Lord, please heal me!"* Instead, he explains why he hasn't been able to reach the solution he's been counting on: *"I have no one to help me into the pool."*

His eyes were so locked on his own understanding of how healing would come that he almost missed the Healer standing right in front of him.

How often do we do the same?

We focus on the *"pools"* in our lives—the solutions we've decided will bring healing or blessing—while missing God standing right in front of us asking, *"Do you want to get well?"* We become so fixated on the path we've imagined that we fail to recognize divine intervention appearing in unexpected forms.

These "pools" take many forms in our lives:
- The relationship we think will bring happiness
- The job promotion we believe will bring security
- The financial breakthrough we assume will finally bring peace

But Jesus' miracles weren't psychological tricks or motivational boosts, as some skeptics claim. The healing of the paralyzed man, like Jesus' other miracles, demonstrated His divine authority and power. Unlike other healers, Jesus didn't pray for God to heal—He healed by His own authority. He didn't suggest or inspire; He commanded genuine physical transformation.

What makes this account so powerful is how Jesus completely bypassed the man's limited understanding. The pool—the very thing he had pinned his hopes on for thirty-eight years—became instantly irrelevant. Jesus didn't help him into the water; He made the water unnecessary.

Perhaps Jesus is standing before you today, asking, *"Do you want to get well?"*—while you're explaining all the reasons your situation is impossible. The solution might not be found in the "pool" you've been watching, but in the God who stands before you with healing that works in ways you never imagined.

Prayer:

Lord, forgive me for the times I've been so fixated on my idea of how healing or blessing should come that I've missed You standing right in front of me. Open my eyes to recognize when You're working in ways that completely transcend my limited understanding. Help me to respond with simple obedience when You call me to "get up and walk" into the future You've prepared. In Jesus' name, Amen.

Courage for One More Step

The LORD himself goes before you and will be with you; he will never leave you nor forsake you. Do not be afraid; do not be discouraged.

DEUTERONOMY 31:8 (NIV)

I stared at the Green to Gold Active-Duty Option acceptance letter in disbelief. As a Private First Class with just 16 months of Army service, I had been selected for a program that would send me back to college and commission me as an officer.

Instead of pure joy, I felt a crushing wave of inadequacy.

There must be some mistake, I thought. *I'm competing against Special Operations Soldiers and senior NCOs with years of experience. How could I possibly succeed?*

The voices of doubt were relentless. I had only just begun to find my footing as an Intelligence Analyst. My uniform still felt new on my shoulders. And now I was expected to lead others? To stand among cadets with far more military experience and knowledge?

Perhaps you know this feeling—standing at the threshold of an opportunity that simultaneously thrills and terrifies you. A promotion beyond your perceived qualifications. A ministry role you feel unprepared to fill. A responsibility that seems to demand more than you have to offer.

Moses' words to Joshua in *Deuteronomy 31:8* offer profound wisdom for these moments. About to lead Israel into the Promised

Land—a task requiring military conquest, governance implementation, and spiritual leadership—Joshua likely felt inadequate for the enormity of what lay ahead.

Moses doesn't minimize the challenge but shifts Joshua's focus to two essential truths: **God goes before him** (preparing the way), and **God remains with him** (providing constant support). These twin realities—divine preparation and divine presence—provide courage not just for the overall mission, but for the immediate next step.

What I couldn't see when I received that acceptance letter was how God had already gone before me. Despite my fears, I not only survived ROTC—I thrived. I ranked #3 in my company and #7 in the entire battalion. The ultimate evidence of God's preparation came when I was selected as a Cyber Warfare Officer—one of only 70 candidates chosen nationwide from a pool that included graduates from Harvard and MIT.

The command *"Do not be afraid; do not be discouraged"* isn't a denial of legitimate emotions but a reminder that fear and discouragement, while natural, need not be the controlling forces in our decisions. We can acknowledge these feelings while still choosing faith-driven action.

What challenge are you facing that seems too overwhelming to contemplate? Instead of focusing on the entire journey, what would it look like to trust God for just the next step?

Remember: He has gone before you, preparing circumstances you cannot yet see—and He remains with you, providing strength you do not yet feel.

Prayer:

Lord, when the journey ahead seems overwhelming, help me focus on taking just the next faithful step. Thank You for going before me and remaining with me every moment along the way. Remind me that Your plans for me are established long before I can see them unfolding. In Jesus' name, Amen.

SECTION V
Cultivating Daily Faithfulness
Theme: Building Habits and Perspectives that Sustain Faith

Small Steps, Big Journey

Whoever can be trusted with very little can also be trusted with much.

LUKE 16:10 (NIV)

When I first arrived at **Army Basic Training**, I was overwhelmed by the transformation expected of me. The disciplined soldier they wanted seemed impossibly far from who I was. My drill sergeant noticed my struggle and shared a piece of wisdom I'll never forget:

"Walker, you don't become a soldier overnight. You become a soldier by making your bed perfectly today, adjusting your uniforms tonight, and being on time tomorrow."

So, I started with small disciplines—waking up five minutes before reveille to center myself, reviewing field manuals during breaks, and perfectly arranging my footlocker. These weren't heroic actions, but their consistent application built the foundation of military discipline.

Spiritual growth follows the same principle. We often desire dramatic transformation, but God typically works through daily faithfulness in the small things. Your brief morning prayer might seem inadequate. That scripture verse you meditate on during lunch might feel insufficient. But these small acts of obedience create the pathway for God's deeper work in your life.

Jesus emphasized this principle of faithful stewardship in the little things. The servant who managed a small amount well was entrusted with more. The disciple who is faithful in small acts of obedience discovers greater spiritual responsibility and lasting impact.

What small step of discipline is God asking you to take today?
Remember, it's not the size of the action but the consistency that transforms.

Prayer:
Lord, help me be faithful in the small daily disciplines, trusting that You're using them to shape my character and prepare me for greater service. In Jesus' name, Amen.

The Rhythm of Rest

Come to me, all you who are weary and burdened, and I will give you rest.

MATTHEW 11:28 (NIV)

As President of the Colorado State Student Advisory Council, I approached leadership with the same intensity that had helped me overcome academic obstacles. Meetings, conferences, policy research, speeches, campus visits—I filled every moment with activity, believing that rest was for those less committed to making a difference.

Then came the day I burned out—just before a presentation to college administrators and the governor of Colorado. I simply couldn't make the meeting. My body enforced the rest I had refused to take voluntarily. That humbling moment taught me something critical: true leadership includes rhythms of rest.

Jesus modeled this beautifully. Despite having just three years of earthly ministry and countless needs around Him, He regularly withdrew to pray and rest. He wasn't ineffective; He was strategic—sustaining His mission through intentional pauses.

In a society that equates busyness with importance, choosing rest can feel like weakness. But Sabbath rest isn't optional in God's design. It's a command equal to the others—a gift that acknowledges both our human limitations and our dependence on God.

Discipline without rest isn't godly discipline—it's self-reliance dressed in spiritual clothing. True discipline respects the boundaries God established for our flourishing.

Where have you been pushing beyond healthy boundaries? What might it look like to incorporate intentional rest into your pursuit of godly discipline?

Prayer:

Lord, teach me to embrace rest as an act of faith rather than viewing it as weakness. Give me wisdom to establish boundaries that honor Your design for human flourishing. Help me find productivity that flows from a well-rested heart rather than constant activity.
In Jesus' name, Amen.

The Unseen Workout

Rather train yourself for godliness; for while bodily training is of some value, godliness is of value in every way, as it holds promise for the present life and also for the life to come.

1 TIMOTHY 4:7-8 (ESV)

The first weeks of military physical training were brutal. While I could manage the running and pushups, building mental toughness proved far more challenging. Our sergeant pushed us to our perceived limits—then demanded ten more repetitions.

"**Your mind will give up before your body,**" he would shout. "**Train your mind to keep going when it wants to quit.**"

I learned to count breaths during the hardest exercises, focusing on just the next inhale whenever my muscles screamed for relief. I practiced mental techniques to push through the discomfort, gradually developing a resilience I hadn't previously possessed.

Paul uses this training metaphor intentionally when discussing spiritual growth. Just as physical training requires consistent effort before results appear, spiritual discipline demands regular practice before it transforms our character. Prayer, Scripture meditation, worship, service—these aren't just religious activities; they are **spiritual exercises** that shape our souls.

The difference? Physical training benefits us temporarily, while spiritual training holds promise for both this life and eternity. The unseen workout of godly disciplines shapes not only how we live now, but also who we become forever.

Are you approaching your spiritual life with the same intentionality as other areas you want to develop? What spiritual "muscles" might need consistent training in your life right now?

Prayer:
Lord, help me approach spiritual disciplines with the consistency and intentionality of an athlete in training. Strengthen my commitment to the practices that shape me into Your likeness. In Jesus' name, Amen.

The Gift of Disruption

> *And we know that in all things God works for the good of those who love him, who have been called according to his purpose.*
>
> ROMANS 8:28 (NIV)

I had done everything right.

I transformed myself academically at the Community College of Denver, graduating with scholarship offers from prestigious universities like USC and Columbia. I even secured a position at a Fortune 500 company. My redemption story seemed complete—I had carefully mapped each step toward the success my mother had always envisioned for me.

Then COVID-19 hit like a hurricane, washing away everything I had built. I lost my Fortune 500 job. The university I committed to closed transfer student housing. While I pivoted to accept a full ride at an in-state college, things continued to unravel. My car broke down. Financial struggles mounted. My girlfriend left me. Everything that had provided stability disappeared—one domino after another.

In those dark moments, I questioned God's plan. Hadn't I already overcome enough? Why more disruption? Why now, when success was finally within reach?

With my options dwindling and family needs increasing, I made a decision that seemed crazy to many—I enlisted in the U.S. Army as an Intelligence Analyst. It felt like stepping off a cliff into darkness.

What I couldn't see then was that this disruption was divine redirection.

My military service opened doors I never imagined. Serving in South Korea, I discovered gifts in intelligence analysis and cybersecurity. I prevented a classified system blackout during a critical military exercise, earning numerous awards and a nomination to commission from a two-star general. Looking back, that COVID disruption wasn't the end of my story—it was God's redirect to a greater purpose I couldn't yet envision.

Disruptions in our lives—whether through job loss, relocation, illness, or relationship changes—often feel like unwelcome intrusions. Yet repeatedly throughout Scripture, we see God using disruptions to accomplish His deeper purposes. Joseph's imprisonment led to Egypt's salvation. Israel's exile produced spiritual renewal. Paul's imprisonment expanded his ministry through letters that would shape the church for centuries.

Romans 8:28 doesn't promise that all things are good, but that God works all things together for good. The canvas of our lives includes both light and dark strokes; it's the combination that creates the masterpiece He envisions.

What disruption are you currently facing?

Instead of merely asking God to remove it, try asking what He might be developing through it. The very circumstance you're praying would end might be the path to purpose you never imagined.

Prayer:

Lord, help me trust Your redirecting hand in life's disruptions. Give me the strength to trust Your work in all things. In Jesus' name, Amen.

Horizons Beyond Home

How many are your works, LORD! In wisdom you made them all; the earth is full of your creatures.

PSALM 104:24 (NIV)

When I was 14 years old, my church "grandparents" invited me on a road trip that would forever change my perspective. Coming from a background of poverty, my world had been limited to my neighborhood in Colorado. But that summer, we drove all the way to Florida, stopping in every major city along the way.

I still remember pressing my face against the car window as we crossed the Mississippi River, gazing in awe at the Gateway Arch in St. Louis, and feeling the humid air of Alabama for the first time. Each new horizon expanded something within me that I didn't even know needed expanding.

For a child who had grown up with limited resources, this journey was more than just tourism—it was a revelation. God's world was so much bigger, so much more varied and beautiful than I had ever imagined. The mountains of Tennessee, the beaches of Florida, the rolling farmlands of Georgia—each landscape spoke of God's creativity and abundance.

In our hustle-and-bustle culture, we rarely take time to simply behold God's creation. We're too busy checking notifications, meeting deadlines, and rushing to the next appointment. Yet Scripture repeatedly invites us to pause and consider what God has made. The psalmist doesn't just acknowledge God's works but stands in awe of their abundance and wisdom.

When was the last time you allowed yourself to be genuinely awestruck by God's creation?

When did you last take a moment to notice the intricacy of a flower, the majesty of clouds, or the vastness of the night sky? These aren't just pleasant distractions—they're sacred invitations to worship.

That road trip taught me that sometimes the most spiritual thing we can do is simply stop, look, and marvel. God's goodness is on display all around us—if only we'll slow down enough to notice it.

Prayer:

Lord, forgive me for rushing past Your wonders. Today, help me pause and truly see the beauty You've created. Awaken in me a childlike wonder at Your works, that I might praise You more. In Jesus' name, Amen.

About the Author

Emanuel Walker's story is one of grace, grit, and divine redirection. Born in a refugee camp during Liberia's civil war and raised by a single mother in Denver, Colorado, Emanuel faced early challenges that could have derailed his future. Struggling academically and battling discouragement, he graduated high school with a 1.6 GPA—seemingly disqualified from the future he dreamed of. But God had other plans.

Through faith, discipline, and a series of unexpected opportunities, Emanuel experienced a dramatic transformation. He became valedictorian of the Community College of Denver, received the New Outstanding Student of the Year Award, and was honored as a Rising Star by the Colorado Community College System. His leadership expanded statewide when he was appointed Chairman of the Colorado State Student Advisory Council, representing more than 127,000 students. He also served on multiple advisory councils under the Colorado Department of Higher Education, helping shape educational policy and access.

Emanuel's impact was recognized nationally when he received the President Obama My Brother's Keeper Award and locally when the City of Denver honored him as an Emerging Leader. Professionally, he has worked with Fortune 500 companies such as Lockheed Martin and continues to serve as a voice for purposeful leadership and systems change.

In addition to his civilian leadership, Emanuel served overseas in the U.S. military as an Intelligence Analyst, gaining a global perspective on discipline, sacrifice, and resilience.

Emanuel writes not from a pedestal, but from the trenches of experience. His debut devotional, UNSHAKEN, is a reflection of the storms he has endured and the faith that anchored him through it all. His passion is to help others discover strength when everything around them is shaking—and to remind them that God's faithfulness is never out of reach.

He currently lives in Colorado, where he continues to lead, mentor, and serve with humility and hope.

What's Next?

Thank you for reading UNSHAKEN: Finding God's Strength When Life Trembles. I hope these devotionals helped you find clarity, peace, and the strength to keep going — even when life shakes around you.

But this is just the beginning.

Stay in Touch:
TikTok & Instagram - @walkwithemanuel

Website:
www.TheWalkerEffect.com
or www.EmanuelWalker.com

LinkedIn:
Emanuel Walker

Support the Mission:
• Leave a review on Amazon if this book encouraged you — it helps others discover it too.
• Share it with someone who needs strength today.
• Join the list at TheWalkerEffect.com to get updates on future projects, devotionals, and content.

We're all walking through something. Let's walk through it together.
— **Emanuel Walker**

Made in the USA
Columbia, SC
05 June 2025

921321c4-e7b8-43c5-b21d-2eec51d2a7d3R01